A Beginner[...]idebook of Hope

by
Jane Peters

Cancer:
A Beginner's Guidebook of Hope

by
Jane Peters

Published by
Encouraging Words Publishing
P.O. Box 356
Lake Hubert, MN 56459

First Printing February 1991
Second Printing (Revised) September 1991

ISBN 0-9628806-0-4
Library of Congress Number: LC# 91-815675

Cover Design by
John and Mary Plein, Golden Oaks Graphics

For your love, courage, support and cheerfulness:
Mom and Elizabeth
this is dedicated to you.

Contents

Introduction

When I told Kenny about this book he said, "Great! I hope I never have to read it!" Me, too. Nobody ever wants to have to meet cancer head on. Even in this enlightened day and age, cancer is a mighty fearful thing. Fortunately, HOPE is a powerful antidote for fear.

Fear can begin to run rampant the moment a family member is faced with a medical report of cancer. For the one diagnosed, there is fear of dying; fear of depleting financial resources for self as well as family members; fear of making an incorrect decision. And, for family and friends, there is fear of losing someone so dear that the thought of not having them in your life is absolutely unbearable.

One of the reasons for this book is to help you look fear square in the eye so you can watch it start to "dissolve". The more knowledgeable you become about your disease and related available treatments, the more fear dissolves. That dark old empty house sitting on the hill can look pretty foreboding in the moonlight. But watch what happens when a stationwagon heads up the drive and a big family spills out and into the house, turning on lights left and right, upstairs and down, while the younger ones run across the yard chasing fireflies, laughing. Same scene, only different. That's what hope does: sheds light where there was darkness. Hope comes from discovering there is reason to hope!

This book also encourages you to stand on the POSITIVE side...the plus side of life...by giving your mind some ideas and thoughts designed to stimulate YOUR own creative take-over process which will result in a more energized, more hopeful you! There ARE options available at this time of crisis. Cancer has been around for so long that there is an enormous, global army of souls dedicated to finding a "cancer control/cure." You will discover people from all walks of life who have had cancer, or who personally know people who have had cancer who are now walking around in a cancer-free/controlled body. Yes, you will also hear of many people who are not alive today because cancer, or the treatment related problems, proved too formidable a foe. But, please remember that even those who have not survived the War of Flesh vs. Cancer have forced the living to try harder, to search more deeply and to NEVER STOP until the plus side wins!

Many members of the human family on this planet are celebrating their personal victory over cancer. They are spreading their messages far and wide, but a starting point of reference is needed so that you can readily find out what is "out there." The fact that you're reading this book is obvious proof that you want to know what's going on! The more you explore...the more you discover. The more you discover, the more you enhance not only your own life but countless others. What you do from here on out will become your own "Living Message." I salute you and wish you Godspeed on your journey.

Jane Peters
1991

Chapter One

The Journey Begins

You have been diagnosed as having cancer and have now entered a totally foreign territory which, I have discovered, can best be approached with a serious sense of adventure. This is not to be construed as a light hearted stance, rather that of earnest exploration. Interestingly enough you are in a position to take this circumstance of events and make of it a powerful, positive experience not only for yourself but for countless others as well. The more knowledgeable you become in all aspects of cancer treatment, orthodox as well as unorthodox, the more you can offer yourself and others. Of course what you will learn will not be confined just to those facing a potential terminal illness. You will become much better equipped to live and love. After all, we are all born to die. What matters is how we live while we're in the process of dying. Too often the shadow is cast before we realize how precious the light.

First off, please realize I understand deeply the initial shock wave that courses through the body upon hearing the words: "I'm sorry, but you have cancer." I know, intimately well, at least some of the feelings you are going through as I, too, have cancer. (Non-Hodgkin's disease nodular mixed lymphoma to be exact.) My symptoms began November, 1988, but were not correctly diagnosed until March, 1989. My personal story to date as published under the title, *Jane's Journal* is included at the end of this guidebook. Right now, YOUR personal experience is important and how you might best take control of what may seem to be an uncontrollable situation. What I've been learning is that there's a lot more happening in the cancer control realm than the average Jane or Joe realizes and the more THIS average Jane learns, the more she wants to share it with others in the same boat, as it were.

From the start I've been working with medical doctors plus alternative treatment specialists. I've also been working with what I call "Nurturians": people who encourage me to nurture my body. Really nurture my body with spiritual, emotional and mental feeding, as well as food, vitamins, exercise, and supplements to help create the most tranquil, happy, healthy me I can be.

As far as "Self Nurturing" is involved I'd say the first step is to utilize your time wisely and well. For me that meant taking a silent retreat. As you'll find out in this book there's a lot of factfinding to be done. A lot of legwork. After a week or ten days of intense information gathering, spending time alone to digest the facts can be very beneficial.

Studies reveal that a typical cancer patient has had a high stress level prior to developing cancer. Stress affects the immune system, the immune system breaks down and somehow, cancer develops. Even if you haven't been stressed out, you're presently in a highly stressful situation because you've just been told you have cancer! How about time for a little break? I heartily recommend you give yourself the gift of at least 24 hours, two days, a week maybe. Alone. Before you go any further on your search, search and research segment say "hello" to yourself. Spend time with yourself somewhere you feel safe and secure. Take time to give the little child in you a big hug and whisper, "I Love You."

Of course right now you might be saying, "Oh sure, Jane, as if I can just drop out of sight right now!! And who's going to pay for this anyhow?" I know it might take some creative finagling on your part, but I'm convinced if you really think this makes sense somehow you'll find a way! Of course, naturally this is strictly optional...well everything in this guidebook is...but I sincerely hope you'll consider at least an overnight silent retreat some place. For me it was pretty darn essential. I've included a chapter on this later in the guidebook, as well as some questions you might want to ask yourself.

Chapter Two

Begin Your Research With Your Doctor

The results are in. Perhaps more tests to follow. At this point one of the first things you might want to do is to get on a first name basis with your doctor. I began calling my doctor "Dr. Jim" before I read that calling doctors by their first name is a real strengthening bond. After all the two of you are sailing through some rough waters right now. Your body is the boat so you have automatically become involved in the decision making. In order to make the best decisions YOU can you should first make sure you have all the facts straight. Even if your doctor is your mother, brother or cherished friend I strongly advise that you get a second (at least) opinion. That goes for the biopsy report as well. You know how we're always being told to get three estimates for the car repairs or new paint job or what have you...well, the same thing applies here. Oh, not for the costs involved, of course, but to reassure yourself that all the facts are consistent. Also, you might want to find out if your doctor has patients with the same type of cancer and "can you please talk to them regarding how they're doing on the treatment program."

It's easy to find out who the leading specialists are in your field of cancer and WHERE they are. Now we begin dealing with something called TIME. Please try not to fall into the trap of believing you don't have any time. It's amazing what 24 hours can reveal. It's O.K., IMPORTANT, WONDERFUL! to be well informed and have as many facts gathered as possible. Your first line doctor should have all the numbers necessary as far as hospitals and clinics in your state that specialize in cancer treatment/programs/clinical trials. If your first line doctor is not an oncologist he/she may not have all the information necessary. Your oncologist will. Whatever you do, GO TO THE BEST! YOU ARE WORTH IT. Once you've found the who/what/where of the best your state has to offer find out the BEST in the region/nation...if necessary the world. For some reason a lot of people believe that it's too much trouble to go out of the county/state for help. Also, there is the understandable sense of loyalty to one's own doctor and state facilities. Doctors and hospitals certainly appreciate loyalty, but they're among the first to make sure you feel free to have second opinions and answered questions! One easy way to start finding out what/where is considered the best is to ask your doctor: "Who would you see if your child/wife/husband/you had cancer? Where would you go? What's the BEST treatment for this type of cancer and where?" Important questions with vital answers. There are some incredible new treatments currently being tested but if you don't know they exist you can't ask about them, can you?

Above all: make sure you know exactly what you are being told. If you don't understand something keep asking questions until you do. A microcassette to record conversations with your doctor can help eliminate confusion as well.

Chapter Three

Pursue Your Own Course of Investigatory Action

There are numerous books in libraries, bookstores and health food stores. Not only by and about people who have "lived to write about" their experiences but also on cancer and cancer treatment programs and choices. The United States has an enormous organization specializing in informing the public on cancer treatment/prevention, et al. Just call 1-800-4-CANCER and you'll get reams of information on the subject! Yes, there's a lot to learn, but before you start throwing your hands up in despair thinking "Oh, me-oh-my, there's too much to have to absorb!", take heart!

It's basically very easy. For starters make a few calls and read a couple of books. The more you find out what's going on the better you will feel. As you'll see, I've mentioned a few "key" books, but remember, this is only meant to guide you on your own personal course of action. Contact any local, statewide or nationwide support group. What videos are available? Publications? Your priority list has changed to reveal that you have embarked on a Research Project. Your mission is to be as well informed as possible on the Who-What-Where of your disease.

One of the things I heartily recommend is to explore the unorthodox. Do I mean stuff like "alternative treatment"...the non-traditional option...the departure from the norm? Yep. You'll be advised by the medical world to have either surgery, radiation or chemotherapy (or maybe all).

A few in the orthodox field will recommend diet and fewer still visualization. The facts are that DIET and SELF-HELP do contribute to the overall well-being of a cancer "patient." Unfortunately, few mainstream doctors know much about nutrition, visualization and the like. Changes ARE taking place, but you have access right now to a lot of potent, powerful information already. Your most immediate "hot-line" to alternative treatment and nutrition guidelines will probably be through your local health food store (or nearest one). All you have to do is say you have cancer, does the store owner/manager have books, information or know anyone in the area who has had alternative treatment? And, bingo. If, for some reason, that comes up empty, there's some information in this guidebook. But of course, naturally, alternative treatment has to be researched as well. It's possible to get patients' names and numbers. If you wish to try anything from a macrobiotic diet to a clinic in Mexico, you MUST CHECK OUT THOROUGHLY whatever program you're embarking on. Good common sense prevails always! Right!?? That means talking to people who are doing what you want to do...or have gone where you are thinking of going!

There are many different types of alternative therapies and that in itself can be a confusing issue; however, the object of this guidebook is to help you form the right decisions and that can't be done without knowing what the options are! Once you start connecting with alternative treatment methods you'll find out that the reason various clinics and methods have been going so strong for so long is because they HAVE success stories. Couldn't be in business without them! A lot of people think of alternative clinics as "Last Hope Resorts," so to speak. There is a change taking place...a slow change but a change none-the-less. Instead of being the LAST choice, some have chosen clinics as a FIRST choice. Many people who intend to have traditional treatment have been opting to spend a few weeks getting "detoxified" in a clinic offering immune system building programs. Most clinics could be considered a crash course in diet and self healing, as well as a non-toxic form of treatment. Of course, need I mention that the majority of the U.S. medical mainstream will think you're bonkers for even exploring alternative therapy; however, there are some hospitals in the U.S. that are taking a much more holistic look at overall treatment as well as fractionated chemotherapy. It's just a matter of finding out where they are. (Check the "Helpful Reading" segment of Chapter Four.)

Some doctors may elect to have nothing to do with you if you choose to "waste your time and money" in such a manner as going to a holistic clinic in Mexico, the U.S., or elsewhere. The main arguments you will hear are: (1) the alternative methods are not "proven" methods and (2) the clinics are just trying to take your money during a vulnerable time in your life. Well, as far as the methods being "proven," I would say check with patients who have a long term "control" rate and as far as costs are concerned, they seem to be pretty much in line. Of course, know what expenses are expected to be prior to going anywhere and make sure you ask questions as to what's covered-or-not to eliminate any "surprises!" Also, there is an insurance company in Texas (Chapter Four, again) which specializes in processing alternative treatment insurance (outside the U.S.) directly with your current insurance holder.

Naturally, alternative treatment centers have patient referral lists, videos, etc. Making the right choice is the touchy part. Interestingly enough, various alternative patients I've spoken to have often mentioned a sense of "gut level rightness" about their choice. I'm sure there are former patients who were not happy with their choice of clinics for a variety of reasons. (I'm sure "traditional" hospitals have their share of that too!) If you do decide to explore unorthodox treatment please don't go after it with the idea it's the cure-all to-end-all. The favorite word you'll be hearing from all medical sectors is "control." Alternative treatment offers a less "toxic" form of control, or if chemotherapy or radiation is used, smaller dosages.

No matter what form of treatment is selected, one basic underlying factor is always constant: NUTRITION. There is a right way and a wrong way to eat. Pure and simple, cut and dried. Some of the "right" ways may be considered extreme for the western culture (such as a strict macrobiotic diet) but well worth exploring as that may be the route with your name on it. Unless your lifestyle is free from sugar, alcohol, tobacco, refined foods, caffeine and red meat you'll have some changes to make. Simply restructuring your diet can make you feel incredibly positive and emotionally ALIVE! Two important ingredients when it comes to decision making. Oxygenate your body with fresh air, exercise and water. Common sense tells you to eliminate all the "good" bad habits you might have. I, too, am extraordinarily fond of certain "sense pleasures" and know just how hard it is to even try to give up some things...but when viewed as a g-a-i-n-i-n-g process it seems to go much easier.

Let's face it. This is the most important decision making you've ever had to deal with in your life. Right? So, what an opportunity to DO IT RIGHT! No matter what you decide to do, you'll be better off in the long run by making dietary and lifestyle changes. And, to date, most information on this has walked the "alternative" line.

There's a rising interest in homeopathy, naturopathy and today acupuncture is as common as chiropractic! Also...do not discount the power of prayer. Even if you're not a believer you have a lot of friends and family who are and they're praying for you. All you have to do is thank them and rest in the fact that this ancient "unorthodox" treatment has been credited with potent results. Really miraculous ones!

Chapter Four

Starting Point

Call, read, write, search and research!
Ask questions, get answers!!

CANCER INFORMATION SERVICE (CIS)
Nation wide telephone service that supplies supportive help along with the most up-to-date information on cancer and local resources. CIS can advise on treatments being conducted around the world, as well as nation wide cancer centers and hospitals. The computerized PDQ, Physician Data Query, provides doctors with active treatment studies as well as a directory of doctors, treatment centers and programs. Your doctor can find the latest information on "your" cancer Pretty Darn Quick!

1-800-4-CANCER

AMERICAN CANCER SOCIETY
National Headquarters:
90 Park Avenue
New York, New York 10016
Check your phone book for local/state listings.
The American Cancer Society conducts basic service programs providing information and counseling services for patients and families. A national organization, it fights cancer through research, education, patient services and rehabilitation programs.

Hospitals and clinics throughout the United States have cancer treatment programs. Some follow the standard (traditional) treatment and others have clinical trial programs or less "radical" traditional treatment such as fractionated-dose chemotherapy (smaller daily doses vs. once a week). In order to be fully informed remember to ask, ask, ask...WHAT, WHERE, WHO, HOW ?

For more information on standard treatment options I recommend Marion Morra and Eve Potts' book, *CHOICES: Realistic Alternatives In Cancer Treatment*. See Page 21.

For information on alternative treatment facilities and doctors, two of the best known cancer information services are:

CANCER CONTROL SOCIETY
2043 North Berendo Street
Los Angeles, California 90027
(213) 663-7801

INTERNATIONAL ASSOCIATION OF CANCER VICTORS AND FRIENDS
7740 West Manchester Avenue #110
Playa del Rey, California 90293
(213) 822-5032

Both the Cancer Control Society and the International Association of Cancer Victors and Friends are informational nonprofit organizations emphasizing nontoxic cancer therapies. John Fink's *THIRD OPINION* (also Page 21 of this guidebook) is THE directory for alternative therapy centers and basic information.

INSURANCE COORDINATORS

(For treatment outside of the U.S.)

NORTH AMERICAN HEALTH INSURANCE COORDINATORS, INC.

5847 San Felipe Road, Suite 4250
Houston, Texas 77057-3062
This company will advise you as to whether your existing insurance will pay for treatment outside of the U.S. I highly recommend you call/write to find out about this program. Don't assume you aren't covered.

(713) 953-0906

Helpful Reading

There are SO many wonderful books for you to discover that this list could take pages; however, here are some "key" cut-to-the-chase books which are available through public libraries.

GENERAL INFORMATION

CHOICES:
Realistic Alternatives in Cancer Treatment

By: Marion Morra and Eve Potts
A great source of information! Answers questions regarding cancer treatments, plus complete listings of where to get help. NOT an "alternative treatment" book from the standpoint of holistic/metabolic/IAT/herbal/homeopathic, etc. These alternatives are within the traditional treatment realm.

THIRD OPINION

By: John M. Fink
FANTASTIC! For people who want to make informed decisions about alternative cancer care programs, support groups and informational services.

(I've just listed these two books under "General Information" because they are so darn informative; however, it's tough for any book to stay totally current that's why I encourage you to ask questions regarding treatment.)

INSPIRATIONAL AND "SELF HELP": THE BASICS

The BIBLE

(Especially Psalms and New Testament)
By: Various Divinely Inspired Authors
Contains many positive statements and eye-witness accounts of "miraculous" healings. Many modern day "spontaneous remissions" have been credited to prayer based on Biblical teachings.

THE CANCER CONQUEROR: An Incredible Journey to Wellness

By: Greg Anderson
A delightful, insightful book. Abigail Van Buren (Dear Abby) says, "This is the first book I have seen that gives those who suffer from cancer, and those who love them, a message of real hope."

LOVE, MEDICINE AND MIRACLES plus PEACE, LOVE AND HEALING

By: Bernie Siegel, M.D.
"Must reading" for every cancer patient, their families and their doctors. More than suggested... required! Dr. Bernie's books have the "ultimate" reading list so no point in my duplicating his suggestions!!

ALTERNATIVE TREATMENT PUBLICATIONS

CANCER CONTROL SOCIETY

Cancer Book House
2043 North Berendo Street
Los Angeles, California 90027
Has full line of books, videos, information and referral service on alternative therapies.

Needless to say, I am not even attempting to list all the books that are available. Healing books geared towards Christian, mystical and metaphysical healing principles abound in copious numbers. You may find yourself led to one or many that literally "speak" to you. Friends and family members may give you a book or pamphlet to read. My suggestion is to at least give it a perusal. There may well be a certain something meant for you to read contained within the pages. You're a researcher now. Search and research. Find out about visualization, the power of positive thinking and the like: incredible support to help you become the best equipped explorer you can possibly be! Again, it's up to you. Isn't that nice to know?

COOKBOOKS AND NUTRITION BOOKS

My, oh my there are a lot of cookbooks and nutrition "guidebooks" out there. The ones I've found helpful include:

BACK TO EDEN AND
BACK TO EDEN COOKBOOK
By: Jethro Kloss (Cookbook based on his work)
(Back to Eden Books, Loma Linda, CA)

THE CANCER PREVENTION DIET
By: Michio Kushi with Alex Jack
(St. Martin's Press, N.Y.)

COOKBOOK FOR HEALTHFUL LIVING
By: Carole Bradford and Beverly Novak (Bradford Foundation, Chula Vista, CA)

FRESH VEGETABLE AND FRUIT JUICES
By: N.W. Walker
(Norwalk Press, Prescott, AZ)

THE HEALING FOODS

By: Patricia Hausman and Judith Benn Hurley
(St. Martin's Press, N.Y.)

LAUREL'S KITCHEN

By: Laurel Robertson, Carol Flinders, and
Brownwen Godfrey (Nilgiri Press, Petaluma, CA)

PRESCRIPTION FOR NUTRITIONAL HEALING

By: James F. Balch, M.D. and Phyllis A. Balch, C.N.C.
(Avery Publishing Group, Inc., Garden City, NY)

I would imagine you can find the majority of the above books in your local health food store. The last thing you need now is to be confused by a zillion different "recommended eating" theories...and the above sampling does, in fact, range from macrobiotic to metabolic and vegetarian diets and concepts; however, there are a lot of good "gems" to be gained from these books. Common sense tells me to eat as if I was in the Garden of Eden. My basic dietary pattern is one of whole grains (including brown rice with every meal) lots of vegetables, vegetables juices, (I'm an avid products. I am not a macrobiotic purist (yet) as I lean more towards a metabolic diet which incorporates more fresh fruit than macrobiotic. Refined foods are definitely O-U-T. Suffice to say, be prepared to change your eating habits for the better. One thing I realized is that as human BE-ings on this planet we are part of the planetary life form and as such function better when we are partaking of our Mother Earth's purest, freshest bounty. We are EARTHlings and are best fueled by whole grains, vegetables, and assorted "fruits" of the earth (which I am sure some will construe to mean fish, chicken and lean meat).

Again, for proponents of books, or authors of books I have not mentioned, this rather small (in comparison) list is meant to help guide readers towards the basic path. Once there the list goes on and on!

F.Y.I.: The books I took with me on retreat were:
THE BIBLE
by Various Divinely Inspired Authors
LOVE, MEDICINE AND MIRACLES
by Bernie Siegel, M.D.
THE ART OF SPIRITUAL HEALING
by Joel S. Goldsmith

Chapter Five

On Retreat

For many this is the first time you've ever given yourself a "mind vacation." A time to rest quietly and BE with yourself. This is meant to be a thoughtful, reflective time. You have had some stunning blows lately. Now, pull in the reins and quiet down. Forget TV, radio, phone calls. Step out of "this world." You will emerge strengthened and more clear headed than you can possibly imagine. I suggest you take with you a book or two. Something that speaks truth to you with a capital "T" as well as a positive "cancer" book. I'll also suggest spending at least ten minutes out of every hour doing nothing but sitting quietly. Yes. Just sitting. Your mind will start to assault you with all kinds of thoughts. Tell them, "SCAT!! Get out of here! I'm not listening to you. I'm just being." Then remind yourself you are just BE-ing. Watch how you start resting in that BE-ingness. You have begun to make a solid connection with yourself and you will be amazed at the relaxation and harmony that will stem out of this. You have entered into a special time beyond words, beyond thoughts and yes, even beyond prayer. This is a time to spend with the special Being that is you.

Unfortunately, however, you may have to grapple with The Personal Guilt Trip. The "if only's" of life. If only I hadn't smoked, drank, ate, drugged, got angry, etc., etc., Well, the fact is you've been given a clean slate. A fresh start. Besides, it's not as if you had another body to be "perfect" with so you could compare now, is it? What's "done is did" and a new day is dawning. Suffice to say you will want to get your immune system (which you will discover in your research to be the life line, so-to-speak, of your body) as strong as possible by eating "right" and eliminating detrimental habits. You know what yours are! If your conscience is pestering you in some area or another, you'll probably have to take the proverbial bull by the horns. The detoxification process is not just for the body it's for the mind as well. Bite the bullet and be brutally honest with yourself. Yes, it might even hurt momentarily but the rewards are beyond description.

You may experience moments of sadness and tears. Not just on retreat, any time. Perhaps you noticed, after being diagnosed, that initially some sort of emotional adrenaline rush occurred. A "We're gonna beat this thing!" attitude and a great one that is, to be sure. But, you may find yourself wrapped up in a spectacular sunset hovering in the distance and suddenly you can't see for the tears. Sometimes the One-on-One of the retreat can bring up emotions that are extremely difficult to feel. When, or if, that occurs one thing I did (and do) is simply think of all the people around the world who are experiencing those same feelings or similar ones and then I feel myself giving out reassuring thoughts and emotional hugs, as it were. Sending my "love and hugs" to all the thousands, millions of nameless, faceless beings who might be experiencing what I, too, am feeling. And you know what? I am comforted! How does that work anyway??

Perhaps you'd like to spend some of your retreat time answering the following questions:

Do You Feel Helpless?

Hopeless? Not in regard to the cancer, mind you. In regard to your personal life circumstances. What makes you feel this way and why?

If You Could Do Anything In the World...

What would you like to do? Have you ever attempted to do this? What is really stopping you? What are your strongest talents? What do you see yourself being: IN YOUR HEART OF HEARTS??

What Do You Like Most About Yourself?

About your life? What makes you smile about your life?

What Do You Dislike About Your "Living" Situation?

If you aren't happy about your home life, why? Have you sought counseling? Why not? What stops you from attempting to make an unpleasant situation better? How long have you allowed old negative patterns to exist? Why?

List Three of Your Good Habits.

How many more can you think of?

List Three of Your "Bad" Habits.

What can you do to change them? Why do you want them?

Would You Like to Live in Another State or Town?

Who, what is stopping you? What would have to happen before you could move?

Do You Feel There's Some Greater Being in Control of Your Life?

Do you spend any time with It? Why not? If you don't believe, are you willing to take a few moments NOW just to "see" if there is some kind of "presence within". (What do you have to lose?)

What Do You Have to Do to Feel "Organized?"

Like clean your drawers, pay your bills, etc.

What Do You Think is Unforgivable About Yourself?

What can't you forgive in yourself, someone else or others? Would you be willing to accept the fact that you are forgiven even your darkest thought the second you forgive others? Would you like to sit for a few moments and experience the forgiveness? Will you?

Retreat Notes

Chapter Six

Jane's Journal

The following details the direction in which I have been personally guided to date as published in the Pequot Lakes, MN., ***Country Echo*** *under the title: "JANE'S JOURNAL."*

Included merely to give insight into the course of action I've been choosing, not neccessarily the course you may wish to follow.

The Country
ECHO
Serving the Cass and Crow Wing County Lakes Area
35 CENTS

Alternative cancer treatment experience chronicled

November 1988

I'm in a Brainerd clinic. Tired. Depressed. Glands are swollen on the right side of my neck. I don't have a cold. They don't hurt. Seems something's going around and swollen glands are a symptom. I'm told to take antibiotics.

December 1988

Same clinic. Different doctor. Glands still swollen. Same diagnosis. Same prescription.

January 1989

It's a busy time. I work for a major Minnesota resort. In addition, I'm a member of the 1989 Minnesota Governor's Fishing Opener Committee. We're gearing up for GFO '89 and things are really starting to move. Glands are still swollen. Time for a third opinion. I also work for a Minneapolis hotel. Seems there's a lot going on. It's almost February before I remember to get that doctor's appointment.

February 1989

Work. Work. Work. New rate sheets. Flyers. Letters. "The Season" is on its way. Big things happening with the GFO as well. I'm helping coordinate the "Shore Lunch" Cocktail Reception for the media in Minneapolis. A preview of the Opener and a sampling of Chef Mitch Omer's culinary artistry. Also, rolling right along with the "Big Fish Banquet", a fund raiser for the opener to be held in March. I have to cancel my first appointment with my Mom's doctor due to a scheduling problem. My next appointment won't be for weeks. I mention my swollen glands to my mother. My mother calls her/my doctor's office and voilà, my appointment is changed to that week. The doctor agrees I have something amiss. He makes an appointment for me with a cancer specialist from Minneapolis.

March 1989

The specialist wants a biopsy of a lymph node in my upper collarbone area. Walk in, get the biopsy done, out type-of-thing. Mayo Clinic Department of Pathology gives my doctor the results. My doctor's office calls. Can I come in the next day? It's Friday, March 17, and Dr. Jim is telling me something he really wishes he didn't have to. I have non-Hodgkin's disease lymphoma. Inoperable. He had the test run twice just to be certain. He gives me an appointment card. The specialist will give me all the details.

Walking out of the office I felt a yearning for a place of worship. I ran through a mental catalogue of churches. Not one seemed right. I thanked God for the Temple of the Earth. Sat still for a few minutes in the car and headed back to work. I decided to first see my dear friend, Liz, at In-Fisherman. She had been most concerned about the biopsy and wanted me to call her right away with the results. I decided to stop in instead. One look and she knew. She gave me a big hug and we went into Al Lindner's office as someone was in hers and Al was gone for the day. I told her what I knew and I wanted to do a run through on her as to what/how I was going to tell my mother and my daughter. Tears welled in my eyes as I tried the words: "I have inoperable cancer."

Tears trickled down my cheeks. I cried. Liz reassured. After a few moments we were smiling the Victor's Smile. She asked if I would like to be alone for awhile. I could stay in Al's office all day and she'd make sure no one would disturb me. She had been reading my mind. I sat still, composed, in a chair facing the window. I rejoiced that I was in the refuge I had been seeking. The list of things to do was scrambled in my mind. I said, "Well, God, You're in full control. What's the first thing to be done?" My closed eyes opened. They landed on a wooden sign hanging next to Al's desk and I read: WHAT WOULD JESUS DO? Confusion flooded out of me on a wave. Order returned. I received direction. First off, back to work. Take care of some things there. Pop in and visit another girl friend in Pequot. Pick up my daughter and go to my Mom's under the pretense of needing something there. Time to get the show on the road. Within ten minutes I was headed back to the resort. My co-workers knew I had run into town for a doctor's appointment and they asked how things were. They responded to the news with an outpouring of support and love. My friend, Molly in Pequot, further strengthened me. I could break the news to my family in the spirit of confidence.

Mom was picking up the newspaper when my daughter, Elizabeth, and I pulled into her driveway. We chatted for awhile and then Mom asked, "What are you doing here?" I replied, "I wanted you both together when I told you the results of the biopsy. It's not good. I have inoperable cancer." Stunned. An involuntary jolt hit their systems. Tears began flowing down my 13 year old daughter face. My mother put her hand over her mouth in disbelief. "You can't have it," she said, "It's impossible!" My daughter sobbed, "Are you going to die?" I told them it wasn't as if we were getting ready to have taps played over my grave. It was a time to pull together, work as a team and get organized. "Don't see me as a dying woman!" I said. "See me in my True Spirit." Now, we've got to hang tough. There may be a lot of changes coming up for all of us. As a family we're all in this together. I'll know more Wednesday morning. You're both welcome to come with me and hear what the specialist has to say. Until then, it's life as usual and I for one am heading out tomorrow as per my plans." They rallied with a massive bound.

I had been waiting weeks to see my song writing partner, Shannon, in her band, "Girl's Night Out". She's married to an old friend of mine and visiting them in Detroit Lakes was always a joy. Grounded in faith, upon hearing of my cancer, they saw me as whole and well and perfect. I felt that way, too. The band was great. Danced all night. Got back to the house in the wee hours and we worked on a new composition until dawn. Palm Sunday, time to sit on the rattan settee and watch the sun rise. A lone oak stood on a gentle hill in the distance. An orange sphere of a sun shone through a sterling silver sky. As it climbed higher it spread itself through the sleeping branches of the oak tree. Then, sunbeams dancing on the frozen particles of air began reaching up, down and through the sun. A huge sunbeam cross blazed on the hill. I turned to Shannon and whispered, "Do you see what I'm seeing or is it just my own optical illusion?" She nodded and replied, "I see it, too." We both spontaneously burst into song: "Praise God from whom all blessings flow..."

I went to sleep and when I got up my old friend, Rod, had a book for me: *The Cancer Prevention Diet* by Michio Kushi. Seems friends of theirs had given them the book a year before. Now they knew why. I brought the book back to show my Mom. It was very informative. The next day she dialed a wrong number asking for macrobiotic foods and ended up talking to Don Heidt of Breezy Point. Seems he had a self healing of cancer of the liver and pancreas 13 years ago using diet and supplements alone. Lots of carrot juice. We met. He advised me as to a dietary (not solely macrobiotic) regime I could begin now. The information he gave me made a lot of sense. Lots of people began giving me names and numbers of other people who had some form of "cancer connection." I began hearing of treatments and hospitals and lifestyles that I had never known existed.

In the meantime, I talked to my best friend, Marianne. We go back to my California high school days and have a strong bond. A corporate executive studying to be a Unity minister, Marianne advised me to get a book: *Love, Medicine and Miracles* by Dr. Bernie Siegel. The morning we talked I was very tired, sobbing, wondering if I even wanted to fight. The past five years of my life had been very hard and sad. She reminded me of my real identity and I knew I could face anything...I was going to enter battle and emerge victorious!!

Clarice Otteson gave my Mom a video of a made-for-TV movie entitled *Leap of Faith*. It's the true story of a woman who cured herself of lymphoma through macrobiotic diet, Bernie Siegel's philosophy of healing, acupuncture and exercise. Her cancer was the same as mine. Different location, but the same kind. When Bernie Siegel came up in the movie I mentioned to my mother that I must buy this book. The next day it arrived in the mail, sent by my sister-in-law, Ginny, who lives in Lake Tahoe. Looks like somebody else had been reading my mind.

The actual terminology for my cancer is "nodular poorly differentiated lymphocytic lymphoma." The specialist informs me that the average life span with treatment is 8 years. I figure, (1) I'm not average and (2) I'm not dying when my daughter's 21. I'm bound and determined to see her raise her own teenagers so I can sit in the corner and gloat! Alternative treatment has been mentioned to me. I've looked into options available. I ask the specialist what he thinks of alternative treatment. He says he's never seen a successful result. I talk to people who have. Two types have been meeting with astonishing success: metabolic and immuno-augmentative therapy (IAT). I discover a massive movement taking place across the United States to bring sanity to the treatment of cancer by using unorthodox methods that are producing incredible results.

Easter Sunday I've arranged to stay at Claire and Craig Nagel's marvelous "Stonehouse." It is time for a silent retreat and there I have privacy, security and beauty. I enter "my" retreat with three books, food to last until Tuesday morning and a change of clothes. It takes me about 24 hours to truly still all my senses. I sit and listen for a long, long time. The second night it thunders.

I've read that stress plays a negative role in your system. I begin a concentrated course of de-stressing. I've also read over and over again how important it is in healing to have fun! I sing and dance a lot, ask for good jokes and exercise for the fun of it! I'm becoming one heck of a good natured being. Killing cancer with kindness. I can almost hear those little half starved cells (which thrive on starches and proteins) saying, "So long, it's been nice visiting with you...We have to go now." I visualize. I see my lymphatic system as one coursing beam of shimmering light streaming through my body. I start to see other people that way, too.

My brothers in California and Nevada are concerned. With the help of Tim Leagjeld and Polly Susens from Pequot, I put together a "Videogram for My Brothers in Westernland." Filmed on the *Miracle Worker* set at Brainerd Community College one Sunday afternoon. In it I chat with them, sing a couple of my recent songs and Mom has a walk on part. The word "cancer" never comes up. My daughter opts not to be involved. She's been in the play nightly and just wants to head home with other cast members after the matinee performance.

Even before the biopsy I had been in contact with friends in the spiritual "healing" consciousness. Soon family and friends were putting my name on local and national prayer lists and prayer chains. From the East coast to the West, prayers were being raised on my behalf in Protestant, Catholic, Fundamental churches and in the metaphysical and mystical communities alike. I received constant reminders that I was being held in prayer. I have so much to be grateful for! My "catscan" looks great, bone marrow checked out. It's localized! All right!!!! I've got group insurance. My life insurance is adequate. I make some changes such as moving out of my apartment into my mother's home. No telling how much work I might miss so I want to cut my overhead. I have a full time job, but no paid sick leave or paid holidays.

The "Big Fish Banquet" was a huge success! I'm busy with projects at work. There's personal business to take care of, too. I need 36 hours in my standard 24. I tell myself to relax. Do what can be done. De-stress. De-stress! I relax.

The facts are: 5 percent to 15 percent chance for a 100 percent recovery. I'm aiming for the Top Ten. Hooray! At least I've got a shot at it. The only treatment being recommended by the medical sector is radiation. My research has shown that cancer research clinics such as American Biologics in Tijuana, Mexico, have been showing impressive results. Smart money says to opt for the cancer "detox" center FIRST, then if the appearance still has to be catered to, go ahead and radiate.

APRIL 1989

I'm excited! This morning, April 13, I find out the group policy where I work will cover the alternative treatment center in Mexico. Plus air fare, plus hotel! That same day at 2pm, I am informed, with other staff members, that our group policy has been cancelled as of 12:01am. I can get coverage under Minnesota Comprehensive Insurance IF I terminate my employment. Then, my existing condition will also be covered. Of course, it won't cover treatment outside of Minnesota. I have talked to friends and strangers who have been to the clinic. I have a gut feeling that the best thing I can do is first go through the course there. Now where/how to get the thousands of dollars I'll need. My mother, Helen Schwartz, is a columnist for the Nisswa Review. She is also an Iowa farmer who has had a couple of back to back drought years. Things are tough for her. She had a stroke last year, diabetes, heart problems. It's enough of a strain just to have a "sick" daughter. She knows how much I want to try alternative therapy. She witnessed the swelling decrease in my neck after only one week under Don's nutritional/diet guidance. She joins me in my conviction. Some of her friends are supportive of the idea, some are not. Neither is my/her doctor. I hate to see her spend her savings on me. Maybe I can sell the "Chester Aquamarine." A magnificent ring. A treasured "heirloom". Now mine to do with as I wish. I do not wish to sell it. I explore the idea of selling it with a buy-back clause. My mother insists on cashing a CD to fund the trip. A businessman in Pequot Lakes hears of my plight and contacts another businessman who offers to lend me money, using the ring as collateral for a reasonable interest and a reasonable amount of time. AGREED!

It's an interesting position. I've had to resign in order to get insurance. No job. No income and not even child support. Insurance premiums, and now a loan to pay. I've asked the company I had been working for if they'll pick up the portion of my expenses that insurance would have covered. They're taking it into consideration.

I've enjoyed working with my fellow GFO '89 Committee members and know it will be a huge success. I'll miss the camaraderie of my company co-workers: Bonnie, Teri, Karen, Wendy and on and on. But, new horizons loom lovingly.

I have my ticket. My medical records. I depart Monday, May 8, for San Diego. I will be met by a shuttle bus which will take me the short drive to the clinic. Treatment will last 21 days with Sundays off. All meals are holistic and will be taken at the clinic. The brochure is potent. The phone conversations with the doctors uplifting. I'm going to get cleaned out!!! I'm aiming for the stars...even if I miss, at least I will have made it to the top of the mountain. And, oh my, what a lovely view!

The Country ECHO
Serving the Cass and Crow Wing County Lakes Area
35 CENTS

Postmarked: Mexico

Treatment begins at alternative clinic

May 8 - May 14, 1989

Minnesota...Monday morning arrived on raindrops. Mom peeked her head into my bedroom. Entering she climbed into my bed, holding me tightly, words of love, hope and encouragement whispering, whispering through the quiet rain. Last minute details. The day flies by and soon I'm on the plane.

Northwest pulled out on time to the minute, climbing out of the rain. Following dinner, shades are lowered for the movie. After a while I feel the urge to raise mine, and there it is. My rowseat mate and I see it at the same time taking a collective breath. There, where pewter cloudland met a twilighting sky, shining through a jagged, gaping cloud hole: a blood red sun. Blood red yet translucent as if stainglass back lit with a mega-wattage bulb. "Have you ever seen a sun that color?" I asked. "Never," he replied. Neither had I. Never, Suddenly I remembered the morning and my mother's words. A deep feeling welling up and overflowing. I stare out the window and catch my tears in a napkin.

California...I spend Monday night in a San Diego motel, the American Biologics shuttlebus picking me up first thing in the morning. That night I rejoice all goes well on the Minnesota homefront. My daughter, Elizabeth, is staying with a family who have a campground on Loon Lake. Their daughter and mine are classmates, churchmates and soft ball teammates. Perfect. My mother has a caring neighbor man who stops by daily, plus she's in close touch with friends. Fine. Everyone's "taken care of." My thoughts are pleasant ones, there is no room for anything else, not even cancer. I go to sleep carefree.

Tuesday...Distant doves are cooing. Flowers and palm trees more than compensate for grey skies. My driver, George, arrives in a comfortable car. We spend 25 minutes on a freeway awash with bougainvilla, oleander, bottle brush trees and eucalyptuses before arriving at the clinic. Enroute I discover that there are 32 states in Mexico and I'll be in the state of Baja, city of Tijuana. I also find out Tijuana means "Land of the Turtles," is ranked as the "World's Most Visited" with 36 million crossing the border annually and this Saturday is the Centennial Celebration.

We arrive at the clinic. Blood is drawn. I'm directed to the charming dining room where I breakfast on fresh orange juice, mangoes, scrambled eggs, wheat toast and herb tea. I have the room to myself gazing over a courtyard filled with flowers and fruit trees. Loquats and lemons, morning glories and roses. Songbirds sing "Bienvenido".

My doctor studied premed and interned in Brooklyn, N.Y. He gives me a check up, reviews my history and starts treatment immediately. First off, I'm "hooked up" to an IV feeding me 25,000 to 50,000 milligrams of vitamin C and B complex. then, B17 (Laetrile) is added. I'm also given a blood thinner, buteric acid for the lymphatic system, and a shot of thymus extract. Plus, I'm to take 45 pills and 10 drops a day. (Most of which I have already been taking for the past month and a half under the nutritional guidance of Don Heidt.)

The "Hook Up" room is a spacious area with 12 grey leather tufted recliners forming a semicircle. A huge television dominates one wall topped with a selection of videos ranging from healing imaging tapes to comedy routines. Any given day there will be 15 to 20 of us in the outpatient clinic, plus an additional 20 in the hospital below.

I've begun to meet some of our fellow "warriors", like John and Pat from Miami. John had a previous history of colon cancer, a colostomy and recently has been diagnosed as having a cancerous tumor on the bronchial pipe leading to the lungs. His session with chemotherapy was devastating to his system. His wife, Pat, remembered a radio program six years ago featuring Dr. Rodrigo Rodrigues, Medical Director of American Biologics. Coincidentally, they met a woman who said they should contact American Biologics. After accidentally meeting her a second time and getting the same message from her they decided to look into it and there they were! He had just completed his three weeks and was getting ready to leave feeling "confident and successful"...and full of good humor. After he leaves I find out John is in the pesticide business. I want to ask him if he feels there could be a connection. I have been informed that my cancer (non-

Hodgkin's lymphoma) has been definitely traced to the herbicide 24D in a study conducted in the state of Kansas.

I also meet Qwyn, from Winnipeg, who will be leaving next Monday. For the past two and a half years she's been in battle. Ovarian cancer, surgery, chemotherapy and now a mass of tumors in her stomach. The Canadian doctors had told her to go home and prepare to die, but the quiet, soft spoken mother of four had other ideas. Through books in health food stores, and talking to people who have had success with alternative therapy she decided to try the clinic. She discussed, with her travel partner, Margaret, the lack of information Canadians receive regarding alternative cancer treatment, a sentiment shared by the Americans in the room over lunch. Thirty countries recognize alternative treatment for diseases such as cancer, diabetes and heart problems.

That afternoon I check into my nearby hotel where a lovely concierge greets me in English with "Welcome Home!" My room faces the pool surrounded with banana trees and hibiscus. Qwyn and Margaret are also staying there and together we walk the four blocks from our hotel to the clinic for dinner. Qwyn has grown fond of Tijuana and talks of moving here. She's happy but she's still "not out of the woods" yet. She gazes at the foothills dotted with homes and says words I have heard often today, "If only I had come here first."

Wednesday...The routine has begun. 8:00 am "hook up" then off to the dining room for breakfast, IV's rolling down the hall or waiting at the table. Buckwheat pancakes, fruit and yogurt, fresh fruit juices, scrambled eggs, omelets, cereal, some or all. Sanka or herb teas. After breakfast it's back to the grey chairs as the IV's drip and Patricia Prince, a ten year cancer survivor gives a talk on destressing. We laugh a lot. Next, Dr. Mike Culbert, Information Director for the clinic continues to regale us with an upbeat talk. Seems adherents of "quackery" such as we are growing by leaps and bounds, and for good reason. The results speak for themselves. Problem is, most people don't have access to the results due to the rejection by the medical world.

We're told positive thinking is no longer theory, philosophy or well wishing, it is a science: psychoneuroimmunology. We're reminded of Norman Cousins' *Anatomy of an Illness* and his utilization of Laurel and Hardy films as a healing factor and how important our emotional state of health is to our own healing. We're also told that one out of three Americans will get cancer. He says this metabolic treatment is not a "cure". This initiates the healing cycle by treating the metabolic dysfunction. "DO NOT DROP YOUR GUARD!!" he warns emphatically. After patients leave there is a strict dietary and nutritional program to follow.

American Biologics works to bring about a balanced body chemistry: homeostasis. A state of ease. When your body is out of whack, you're diseased. Biochemistry symphonicly arranged is the result of proper vitamins, minerals, enzymes, amino acids and hormones.

We also find out that:

*What you eat and what you think does TRULY affect your body.

*Your basic health is more important than the bacteria you're incubating, that's why it's more important to build the host (your body) line of defense.

* No two treatment are alike because no two metabolisms are alike.

* Cancer and heart disease are very easy to prevent and very difficult to treat.

* And...this interesting observation: "Cancer is a 'non-uterine' pregnancy incubating cancer...as if a new being is developing outside of time and place."

We listen attentively when he says that alleopathic (traditional) treatment of cancer is cut, burn and poison. Adding that 55,000 deaths in Viet Nam turned Washington, D.C. around, but the 550,000 annual deaths by cancer are not making a dent in the treatment method. Why aren't cancer victims taking to the streets the way AIDS victims are, he wondered out loud.

The rest of the week...everything is a series of highlights like:

Linda...Beautiful, bubbly wife and mother of two from New York, the epitome of fearless chic, whose breast cancer was treated with surgery and chemotherapy before given the "go home and die" directive. She's been here before and comes back for periodic treatments. She's familiar with the lay of the land and we hop "downtown," on Mother's Day, May 10, in a 30 cent per person taxi, taking in the sights like real tourists.

Mike...A Viet Nam vet, California resident, victim of MS caused (both he and his neurologist feel) by Agent Orange. Before he came to A.B. he couldn't raise his arms, or even move his wrists to any degree. He reached for the ceiling effortlessly..."See, I'm doing great! The V.A. Hospital couldn't help, and of course the government won't pay, but I'm coming along fine!!" He picked up his cane and walked proudly out of the room.

Ben...A retired Kentucky coal miner here with his wife and two grown daughters. He has recently been diagnosed as having cancer of the liver after having cancer of the gallbladder. The family made A.B. their choice after talking to two people in their county who have had successful results here. This family is always smiling and chuckling with and over "daddy."

Church bells waken me at 7 am, preceded by a back yard rooster. Days are falling easily into place. There are 12 other alternative clinics in town and I'll be touring them next week. The basic premise of this clinic is, of course, crisis management, but perhaps more importantly, it is an information center. Technology exists to help people NOW prior to getting cancer. However, we all know "well" people don't spend money like "sick" people have to. American Biologics and other established "alternative" clinics are conducting research programs to successfully:

1. Detect cancer early

2. Treat it early

3. Prevent it from developing open tumors

There's a lot more to discover. Best of all, I'm surrounded by people who are standing firm in and on The Word. Everywhere I look I see love pouring out of eyes. As the week winds to an end, I wonder how the Opener's coming along! I have a feeling everything's fine!

The Country
ECHO
Serving the Cass and Crow Wing County Lakes Area
35 CENTS

The Choice:

Laetrile therapy among the unorthodox treatments

May 15-21, 1989

Monday: I'm thinking it's pretty incredible. Back home in Minnesota I can buy an abortion, cigarettes and alcohol...but I can't buy apricot pit extract believing it can prolong, or even possibly save my life. Something's amiss.

Kernels from the apricot pits are processed into a liquid or tablet form called Laetrile, vitamin B17, amygdalin, or natriloside and at this minute some is drip, drip, dripping into my vein. Funny I had to come to Mexico to find out Minnesota has been in the "Laetrile War" since the mid-70's when two Rochester health food store owners were charged with receiving it in the mail. Hubert Humphrey responded to the entrapment arrest by calling for an FDA hearing on Laetrile in light of the continued favorable comment on its effectiveness by users. Basically Laetrile contains cyanide which is released only in the cancerous cells and its efficacy works hand in hand with proper nutrients in the body. That's why diet, vitamins, plus mineral supplements are so vital to the treatment process.

Since live-cell therapy is also a part of the individualized metabolic program Dr. Wolfram Kuhnau is giving a lecture on what live-cell therapy is all about. Kuhnau, an articulate, handsome 79, is one of the original disciples of the late Paul Niehans, father of cellular therapy. Niehans patients ranged from Charles DeGaulle and Dwight D. Eisenhower to Charlie Chaplin and Sir Winston Churchill. Perhaps the most famous Niehans patient of all was Pope Pius XII who, while dying, summoned Niehans to his bedside for injections and went on to live four more years.

Live-cell treatments are a combination of endocrinological stabilization ("hormonal harmonizing" Dr. Kuhnau calls it) rejuvenation and regeneration. All treatments consists of intramuscular injection of cellular suspensions from calf embryonic endocrine glands and other tissues. I'll receive my first live-cells tomorrow. The clinic's been incorporating live-cell therapy with remarkable results for cancer patients and neuromuscular disorders (Parkinson's disease, post-stroke paralysis, MS, etc) as well as dermatological disorders, hormone dependent dysfunctions (the clinic has two babies to its "credit" after treating two Canadian women for infertility), genetic and hereditary disorders and others, as well as allergies.

Bea's here because of her allergies. This pretty, petite wife and mother from South Dakota has Universal Reactor Syndrome. In a nutshell, she's allergic to the 20th century! The siege began four months ago when her immune system went berserk, leaving her looking like a scald victim, red, peeling from head to toe and allergic to just about EVERYTHING! After two U.S. clinics and a loss of 30 pounds from her 5 foot frame, a doctor from the second clinic recommended she try American Biologics. Two days after her live-cell injections I noticed a marked change in her appearance, best of all she was feeling better and encouraged with the results to date, especially after so many months of just watching her condition worsen with no end in sight.

Kathy, a vivacious nurse from New York is here on a "six month maintenance" program for her anemia and allergies. She had learned about the clinic through a health magazine and since she had not been meeting with much orthodox success, she decided to give it a go. She's sold on the program and doesn't even bother to explain to the medical establishment what she's up to as they have so little tolerance for alternative treatment. As she points out, she's not going to stress herself out trying to convince people that the treatment's effective...she's living proof and that's all that matters.

Kathy's hospital roommate, Jan, is on her way back to New Zealand. She's one funny, spunky lady and I hope someday our paths will cross again. It's hard to believe that once she was bedridden with lupus and unable to even hold a cup in her hand. This was a "follow up" short stay for her. The first and last time she was here was in late Fall of last year. She first heard of the clinic two years ago but was reluctant to "lurch across the world in search of a miracle cure." However, she met a fellow New Zealander who spoke highly of the clinic so she decided to at least give it a try. Up until then she had been on heavy steroids leaving her with a huge moon shaped face reducing her eyes to narrow slits. Her home life on the "farmlet" suffered serious damage as well.

After receiving live-cell metabolic treatment she headed home being advised that it would be six weeks before she saw any measurable results. She waited eight weeks before...RESULTS!! Swelling subsided, movement improved, she was returning to normal! She told a New Zealand newspaper reporter, "I'm still on steroids, although the dose is much lower than before and I consider there is still a long way to go before I am cured. But this program has worked wonders. I can't say enough about it and the other marvelous results I saw, especially among cancer victims. For me it's just a matter of time, more therapy and a wait and see approach. But life's a smorgasbord out there and I want to taste more of it."

Another good bye. This time to the stunningly beautiful Tracey from Lake Tahoe. The 25 year old had been here for four days hoping to hear a different diagnosis than the one already received from her doctor back home. The clinic had confirmed the recommendation: surgery for cervical cancer. Tracey wanted children. Five years ago her mother died from cancer leaving Tracey to raise her 15 year old brother. She sparkles and says she's optimistic. She shows me a picture of her dog. And her boy friend. I see my daughter in Tracey and we hold each other tightly saying good bye. In her eyes I see Tracey wanted children.

Just because this clinic specialized in metabolic treatment doesn't mean that surgery, chemotherapy or radiation aren't recommended if necessary; however, dosage may differ from state side practices. George had some chemotherapy during an earlier stay. His personal saga includes first being treated in Michigan for a blood clot in his throat. When he lost his voice a tumor was discovered pressing against his voice box. Then, chest tumors. The tall, genial McGuffeys's Home School publisher and father of five first arrived at the clinic with his wife, Jackie, last December. At the time he spoke with a high pitched "squeak," had tumors on both lungs and in the center chest area. When he left, the lungs were clear, center tumor still there, and the voice still out-of-order. Back home a "miracle" occurred regarding his voice. One weekend they noticed his voice was "breaking". That Sunday, after church, a friend of theirs called saying she had been watching the 700 Club on Friday and Pat Robertson was saying that a man "out there" had a tumor on his vocal chords, God was healing him and everything was going to be fine. The friend said she knew George was that man. Two days later, during lunch, George's voice suddenly returned to normal!

George was feeling SO good he decided he could stop taking his heart medication. His body rebelled and once again George and Jackie returned to the clinic. This time with wheel chair assistance. The bottom third of his lungs showed tumors again. The center tumor was enlarged. That was four weeks ago. Tomorrow new x-rays. One thing's for sure...he's looking good and getting around just fine now. George and Jackie have a love for each other and God that's a joy to witness.

Dr. Robert Bradford, former Stanford engineer, physicist and founder of the Bradford Research Institute which supplies the clinic all the state-of-the-art technology and modalities available from research around the world is actually giving me a blood test. Quite an honor! Plus, the test is fascinating. Prick the finger. Drops of blood on the glass slide. Slide under microscope, turn on the TV (!) and there they are—my red blood cells, white cells, "stuff in the blood." All enlarged, moving and in living color. He tells me what I'm seeing and I sit entranced. Every doctor's office should have one of these babies!

I got my first live-cell injections. I'm to rest.

Peter, a New York journalist with Universal Reactor Syndrome, and I are both hoping the sharks will arrive soon. We want shark live-cells!! I had first heard about some remarkable studies involving shark cartilage in the treatment of cancer through Wes Anderson of Nisswa. I had requested to be selected as part of the experimental program here administering embryonic shark live-cells and was tickled to hear Peter was also vying for them. It's a go!!! Looks like Peter will be #31 and I will be #32 patient to receive shark live-cells in the two years since Dr. Kuhnau first experimented on himself. The shipment should arrive tonight and, after processing the embryonic cartilage and umbilical cord, live-cells will be ready by Friday. Sharks are the healthiest creatures going. They CANNOT get cancer (or AIDS). What happens is simple: when shark live-cells are injected into the human body, the blood supply feeding the cancer is cut off. Simple. Sounds too good to be true? Well, I for one am thrilled at the prospect of being Guinea Pig Peters. Wonder if I'll swim better.

Wednesday: Hook up. Drip...drip. Eat...eat. Maria, the dietician, is some kind of woman! She oversees a kitchen which turns out the finest soups, entrees and healthy food you ever did see. We're talking highly vegetarian here though. Don't expect any steaks or fried food. I didn't know you could cook vegetables so many ways. Spaghetti with artichoke hearts and carrot sauce was an all time first. Whole wheat spinach spaghetti noodles at that. And you know what? It was really good.

Mike, a nutritionist Ph.D., who last year recovered from Epstein-Barr is here today for a weekly drop-in "drip." This is part of his on-going total wellness program and he swears by it. He's a busy guy. Partner in a major national cosmetics firm and lecturer on nutrition, he wants to stay as totally together as possible!

I wanted to see some other clinics this week, but so far I've been on a "quiet program" for the live-cells and haven't been able to hop around the way I'd like. Looks like I'll have to wait until after the weekend to see what some others are like. The only two I'd ever heard about were American Biologics and the new IAT clinic. Once here I find there are others which have a following as well. The Hoxsey Clinic is known for it's tonic. Seems Hoxsey used to be widespread in the U.S. but the FDA "ran them out"; however, from the huge number of adherents to the Hoxsey formula I gather there's something special in the herbal blend. I'd also like to pay a visit to Contrerus Hospital, the pioneer Laetrile clinic.

There are a number of clinics and hospitals in the United States that combine traditional and holistic treatments, but they can't use Laetrile. Some of the ones mentioned to me back home had been American International in Zion, Ill., the Cleveland Center, the Cancer Counseling and Research Center in Texas as well as the work being done by Stanislaw Burzynski, also of Texas. He is widely supported by his patients in his efforts to legalize the use of his non-toxic antineoplaston therapy. Unfortunately those thousands upon thousands of us opting for alternative treatment are blocked from receiving it due to the FDA and medical monopoly. A few states do allow doctors to give Laetrile to their patients as long as it's for the "patient's well being...and not cancer." Laetrile "controls" vs. cures, similar to insulin for diabetics. Many have called the "cancer industry" irresponsible in disallowing the "unofficial" clinical evidence for the efficacy of B17. One day things will be different.

Thursday...Friday...The rest of the week...sees me daily greeting many of the same faces I saw when I first walked in. Janice and Bud, from St. Petersburg, Fla., share a special glow. Janice had two cancerous tumors removed from her breast in October of 1987. She knew there was still something wrong but the mammograms were negative. She should have been fine. Janice kept insisting something didn't "feel" right. Even Bud said she must be fine because the mammograms were fine. She asked for a mastectomy. Why?? The mammograms were FINE!!! In September of 1988 her breasts were hard and discolored. Almost overnight. Finally someone listened. She had a double mastectomy plus a massive amount of muscle tissue had to be removed. Radiation was given. For weeks on end. More tumors began developing and Janice and Bud decided to leave the orthodox medical world. First the Everts Clinic in Alabama, then American Biologics. Bud's face reflects loving devotion to his wife when he says, "I just wish we'd been here two years ago."

Two other couples share the bond of marriage "made in heaven". The two women are sisters, Helen and Erica, from British Columbia. Both have cancer. Each couple is united with such a beautiful spiritual essence that they raise my heart as well. Last week Helen had an unusual reaction to a chest IV (called a subclavian catheter). While it was being inserted she suddenly went into shock. Her heart stopped. Immediately she was revived by the medical team. I visited her briefly the afternoon it happened. She looked at me, blue eyes twinkling, telling me where her "health" truly lies. Nothing's stronger than faith! Her husband, Peter, sister and brother-in-law Robert, had met the crisis with such composure and strength that I saw a mountain being cast into the sea.

*George's x-rays are looking good! Still has a way to go...but getting there!

*OH NO!!! The sharks may not be here 'til next week. Pete and I discuss taking in a bullfight...I'm leaning more towards the Cultural Center and Omni theater!

*My doctor, Dr. Alzate, is happy my tests look so good. I ask him if I can live to be 100. "That's fine with him," he says. Me, too!

*I miss my daughter. School's going to be out and I won't be able to hug her and say "Good going, Liddybeth!"...or say goodbye to the Pequot teachers.

*What wonderful cards, letters and words of encouragement I've received! I am so thankful and feel so, well...WELL!!

The weather's been better in Minnesota than in Mexico. Haven't seen sunshine for days and I've had the heat on in my room many a day. However, I am warmed by the companionship and friendship of all my fellow "alternative choicers" and their family and friends. I'm also warmed by the people of Tijuana I pass daily walking to and from the clinic. I'm on a regular schedule, just like the rest of the working force and familiar faces have replaced those of strangers walking, or watering the garden, or sending the children off to school. I'm warmed by the staff and employees of the clinic who call me "Juanita", Spanish for Jane, who treat all of us as if...well, as if we are people destined to live long, happy lives.

The Country
ECHO
Serving the Cass and Crow Wing County Lakes Area
35 CENTS

The Results Are...

Alternative treatment concludes in Mexico

May 22-29

Monday: There are plastic "patches" on my neck and collarbone, the confined area of cancer in my body. Wires run to a machine. Another patch is on my leg acting as a ground wire. Why am I looking like the Bride of Frankenstein, IV dripping on one side, wires running out of the other? I'm getting a positive charge. White blood cells are a negative charge, cancer's a negative charge so the trick is to change the negative cancer charge to a positive one so my immune system can start getting to work.

You see, as far as it's concerned there's nothing to fight ...I'm cancer free! But my doctors know, and I know, I'm not.

The actual term for this is bioelectrical therapy or ACN: accelerated charge neutralization. It's the electromagnetic probing of malignant tumors by which the static charge is altered, circumventing one of cancer's primary defense mechanisms.

I've been advised to get a couple of mercury/amalgam fillings in my teeth replaced as they are emitting a powerful negative charge and that could be contributing to the inability of my own defense system to kick in properly. Short circuited, so to speak. I began explaining this "current affair" to a young California couple, Blake and Lisa, thinking I must sound rather flake-o and discover this isn't news to them. Blake, who has widespread lymphoma, had all of his fillings replaced months ago by the leading "expert," Dr. Huggins in Colorado Springs. Seems a lot of people are aware of this connection and even the healthy-types are replacing their filling with non-current conducting material.

It's gorgeous and sunny and warm and it was so-o-o-o good to see Bill walk into the hook-up room today. Last week was a rough one for him and the contrast was remarkable. His delightful wife, Kim, flashed a smile to everyone in the group. I could sense her relief as well. The Steven's Point, Wisconsin, couple and I have grown close...midwestern neighbors that we are. A month ago Bill was diagnosed as having pneumonia. A closer look revealed cancer: lungs and kidney. His doctors told him there was nothing they could do, he had, oh, sixty days or so...so why not go home and...Well, this couple (who recently celebrated their first wedding anniversary) had other ideas. A friend of theirs was at the clinic three years ago for leukemia and is doing fine today. They gave him a call. An American Biologics brochure was in the Wellness Section of their hospital (!!!). He's not running at 100 percent by any means, but he figures he has nothing to lose and everything to gain by TRYING! "Besides," said Kim, "the attitude alone here is worth it. Everyone of the doctors back home were so negative. Here there's a positive aspect."

It's tough on the patients but, in my book, family and friends have an equally hard row to hoe. Jackie, a lovely store owner from San Francisco whose husband Jim is being treated here, was telling me about her support group while we were "clinic hopping" yesterday. (She also told me I smell like corn-on-the-cob boilng in a pot. A Laetrile side effect. Oh well, pass the sea salt.) Jim's an executive who also races his own Formula Ford sports car. He had some back pain last year. The diagnosis was a degenerative disc. While getting an eye exam his opthomologist saw something suspicious and recommended Jim get some x-rays. Lung tumors were revealed and surgery was scheduled. The night before surgery his oncologist called saying she remembered Jim's passing statement regarding some back pain and wanted a base-line bone scan done prior to surgery. Results: tumor on the spine. Surgery was out, chemotherapy and radiation were in. Things seemed O.K. Just this March he finished seventh in a race. Within weeks brain tumors were discovered. Radiation and more radiation.

When they decided to go south-of-the-border for treatment Jim's radiologist replied with an unusual response: "Go for it! Let's hope it works!" It's a rare doctor indeed who concedes that "in some cases" alternative treatment "just-might-possibly-be" effective. Alternative choicers are the first to recognize that all forms of cancer treatment can be allies. The "cut, burn, poison" of surgery, radiation and chemotherapy have an important role to play as do psychotherapy and the entire range of alternative treatment.

I had been told the best therapy for my form of cancer is radiation. My doctor at this "alternative clinic" had also said radiation is excellent for localized lymphoma; however, confirming what I had already learned, the FIRST choice is to see what the body's own defense system (the immune system) can do prior to radiation. Besides, the stronger my own line of defense, the more rapid my recovery and, hopefully, the less chance of it popping up elsewhere. Makes sense to me.

Now, if we can get this positive charge to take hold!

Tuesday: Kathleen's getting "charged" today, too. She's already noticed a diminishing of her breast tumor and is obviously quite happy with the results. A retired French teacher from Rhode Island, Kathleen's been aware of alternative treatment for years. Matter of fact, when cancer was first suspected she told her doctor, "Well, you know where I'm going, don't you?" Indeed he did. Ten years ago Kathleen's husband, a Brown University History professor, died from cancer. She attributes his prolonged life span and, thankfully tremendous pain relief, to the Laetrile injections which, with great trouble, she was able to obtain through the then "Minnesota Underground". "Fortunately," she said, "It's much easier to obtain nowadays." She added that alternative therapy is still quite the taboo subject in Massachusetts and Rhode Island. "The Midwest and West are much more receptive to this form of treatment."

*There are a lot of new faces. The hospital is full. One new arrival is Miguel, an adorable boy from Monterrey, Mexico. His mother and father are the picture of Spanish aristocracy. Miguel has Down's Syndrome and is here for live-cell treatment. The clinic is gaining quite a reputation for encouraging results in this area.

*Julie came with her dad. This pretty 24 year old New Yorker was invaded by MS a couple of years ago. She decided on the clinic after talking to a man who had dramatic results with his multiple sclerosis after treatment here. The Big Mac-Burger King-Wendy's-Pizza kinda gal is not too keen the vegetarian fare. She's vowing to eat her veggies, like it or not. Ah, what price wellness.

"Wellness," we're reminded is a combination of a total nutritional diet, exercise, good "habits" and a positive mental attitude. The latter playing a massive role in the overall picture. While there is no "required" reading here, popular books include "Getting Well Again," "Love, Medicine and Miracles", "Love is Letting go of Fear", Louise Hay's works, books by American Biologics own Dr. Wolfram Kunhau and Mike Culbert...The Bible...and a cookbook, "Ten Talents" by Dr. and Mrs. Frank Hurd from Minnesota!

The mental aspect of healing is one I take to heart. Since goal setting is important to reaffirm life I start making a list. Just when I'm thinking about some unfinished goals and dreams in Hawaii who should walk in but Don from the Big Island! I hadn't know him personally, but was well acquainted with his mega-souvenir business. He has a macadamia nut farm and is distributing to health food stores. (Macadamia nuts are an excellent source of Laetrile). Don's here for Chelation therapy, an IV circulation treatment many heart patients swear by claiming it helps them "bypass the bypass."

Talking with other patients we discuss what we do for ourselves for FUN!!! I thought about my one week vacation at the end of January during which I worked on some potential income producing projects while weathering the roads from the Brainerd Lakes Area to Grand Forks to Minneapolis. I did visit with friends enroute, but there was a lot of rush-rush and let's hope the car starts type thing the entire time. I enjoyed some "fun" volunteer projects with the local little theater; however, I see in the future I must study "The Art of Having Fun" a little more closely.

Stress, and its relation to cancer is stressed (no pun intended) over and over again. The secret is to be stress free in a stressful world. The old immune system can only take so much. Dr. Kuhnau, the famed live-cell therapist here, also mentioned that a common trait among cancer victims is a blow to the head or a black-out sometime in a patient's life. Live-cell injections help restructure the damage.

There's so much to learn. I'm glad I've come. What a vast amount of information I can pass along to my daughter (whether she realizes she's getting it or not!) Too bad we don't have mandatory classes in "How to Live Before You Die". Sort of a "Build and Protect the Immune System"...The National Body Guard.

Wednesday: Routine IV hookup. Breakfast, "zap" time for a couple of hours on the bioelectrical machine (I don't feel a thing). Time to reflect on:

*The music and singing everywhere. A wonderful nurse, Elias, always has a happy tune on his lips. Mariachi bands perform in nearby restaurants and the melodies float down the street and up through my bedroom window. I've changed rooms so I could "...lift up mine eyes unto the hills." The little maid sings happily while she cleans.

Then again...

*The other day the "Wisconsin Kids" and I took a drive down the Baja Peninsula. Coming back through Tijuana-town some cars behind us started honking their horns, passing us by, zig-zagging through the on-coming cars. Traffic halted as a car ahead of us was surrounded by men and women holding rifles! I looked at the floor board and knew where I was heading if I heard anything even faintly resembling gunfire. The only uniform was a cap. I figured they were the "good guys". I was right. Problem is, they stopped the wrong car and lit out as if they were being filmed.

*Which is what's happening down the street from my motel. A Mexican film crew is busy working daily on some sort of "border-drug-action" movie. Most of the cast and crew are staying at the motel, but schedules are such that I have yet to be discovered.

Thursday: Pearl and Eddie are also staying at the motel and this morning I took the shuttle to the clinic with them instead of walking. Eddie has cancer of the throat and mouth. His speech is impaired, but he's here hoping he won't have to have more surgery which will leave him mute. Hope seems to be one of the greatest survival skills going. Opponents of alternative therapy claim that "false hope" is often given to desperate victims of disease. I did not find that to be so and after asking others here, find no one else feels anything akin to "false hope" was implied prior to or after admission.

Butch's doctor in upstate New York told him his case was hopeless. "Where there's life...there's hope", said his wife Jeanne. A series of events led to Butch's sister, Linda, talking to a number of people, including Don Heidt of Breezy Point. One man in their hometown had been to Tijuana twelve years ago and was doing great, so they had some "living proof" at hand.

Butch is an in-patient who, after a malignant kidney was removed, was informed everything was fine. There was no follow up treatment such as chemotherapy and frequent check-ups confirmed everything "was great."

Eight months after surgery Butch began having pain in his back, ribs and elsewhere. A CAT scan revealed cancer. Renal cell. Incurable. Radiation eased the pain. Interleukin-2, the then-heralded "magic bullet" was used. He was told he'd be bedridden the rest of his life. A nurse suggested a body brace so he could at least get around in a wheelchair. They were able to get him on the plane and down to Tijuana. In many cases the only ammunition left in the arsenal is alternative treatment...and prayer. One thing's for sure, Butch, Jeanne and Linda, plus the family and friends waiting back home, are not going to let cancer get the best of them...Not without a knock-down-drag-out-no-holds-barred WAR!

As the final week comes to an end...

A new blood test reveals I'm healthier than when I walked in (and that was pretty darn healthy). But..."IT'S" still there. I do notice a difference: the lumps are somewhat smaller. I will be the first to say that prior to the bioelectrical treatment I really hadn't noticed any difference at all. It will be interesting to see what my Brainerd doctor thinks.

The basic premise of my treatment program has been to build and strengthen my immune system and attack the cancer by feeding my body enzymes which break through the protective halo of protein surrounding the cancer enabling the Laetrile to enter and destroy with cyanide. This is coupled with vitamin IV's, dioxyclor IV, a shot of thymus extract, butyrate, and vitamins and minerals which I take orally. Plus, live-cell injections and bioelectrical treatment. The time has come to get more aggressive.

My doctor here (who left orthodox oncology for alternative treatment) would like me to begin a radiation program at this stage of the game. Of course I will be taking Laetrile, vitamin C and other vitamins, minerals and nutritional supplements before, during and after treatment. Ruth Mills, of Breezy Point, has already suggested her radiologist and I know Minnesota doesn't lack for excellence in that field. I have a suggested radiation program in hand but am reminded to listen to what my Minnesota radiologist has to say.

I've seen enough encouraging results to believe this form of treatment should be available to all people everywhere as a first, supplemental or last line of defense. It is now, of course, but it entails having to travel far from home, frequently facing ridicule from some sectors of the "civilized" world. From what I've seen, I can't understand what the big fuss is all about anyway! Some people may not respond as well as others (but isn't that true in the "medical" world as well?); however, live-cell therapy aside, we're just talking about some vitamins, enzymes and minerals. What's so threatening about that? And why not give people the option without having to leave the U.S.? Most of all, if this "quack stuff" doesn't work...how come I've met so many people in the last three weeks who are living proof it does?? I have a sneaky feeling that if every doctor in the U.S. spent ten days of their life going through alternative treatment, finding out first hand what it's all about, they'd be able to keep their patients healthier, happier, longer...not to mention themselves!

Cancer is called the disease of civilization. I, for one, hereby gladly resolve to engage in a primitive lifestyle of eating nuts, berries, fruits and vegetables coupled with laughter, play and love. Being "sick" is too darn expensive and there are other things to do in life...like writing songs about The Great Healer. It's time to start thinking about getting packed. Some of my alternative choice friends are concerned about my getting radiation. The ones who are, are the ones who have.

I've had an interesting last minute proposition. The response to the bioelectrical treatment has been so good that the research department at the clinic has asked if I would like to stay for another week, gratis, as they are interested in watching the continued results. I'm tempted. I consult with my doctor. He confirms there has been a change and it's up to me of course; however, he says that after six more days he would most probably stand on his recommendation for some radiation. Right now it's in a vulnerable state...I'm in great shape to radiate.

I agree.

Besides...I'm homesick.

The Country ECHO
Serving the Cass and Crow Wing County Lakes Area
35 CENTS

Update:

Return to the states, more cancer testing

May 30-June 7, 1989

Tuesday: May 30... Return to verdant, flowering (albeit grey skied) Minnesota and the welcoming arms of family and friends. I feel strong, "good stuff" pumping through my veins. Time to approach the next course of action. Start at the University of Minnesota. The radiology department comes highly recommended. I make an appointment for Friday.

Friday, June 2...Consult with radiology oncologist. They want to do a lymphangiogram to make sure my abdominal nodes are cancer free. "No problem," I reply. "I've already had a CAT scan there and got a clean bill of health!" "Sorry, Jane," they say. "A CAT scan doesn't pick up abdominal nodes." Oh. Hmmmmmmm. Nobody ever mentioned this to me before. Another fact to file: If I ever get nodular poorly differentiated lymphoma again, make sure a lymphangiogram is done. O.K., what else? Head scan. Fine... when? Monday. Tuesday and Wednesday the lymphangiogram... and we'll make an appointment for you at the dentist. Routine prior to radiation.

Monday: June 5...Head scan.

Tuesday: June 6... A needle shoots blue dye between a couple of toes on each foot. Novocaine on top of feet. Small incision made. Find the lymph glands (that's why the blue dye) place tiny IV needles in them and feed poppy seed oil based fluid into glands for say, oh, an hour and a half. Needles out, stitches in. Clear liquid diet all day.

The phone rings that afternoon while I'm sipping on some broth. It's Dr. Bradford from the clinic in Mexico! How am I? What's going on? He had been presenting a paper in New York when I left the clinic and returned to find out my doctor had dismissed me recommending radiation. That doctor is no longer with the clinic. Radiation would be/is counterproductive to the treatment I had been receiving there! My live cells are just beginning to take hold. Of course he understands it's difficult to be patient when there are still some signs of the disease and, naturally, I must do what I feel is right. I tell him I'm just getting more tests done. I feel great! I don't want to mess up what I've done to date, either... and, by-the-way...just before I left Mexico I happened to notice a couple of paragraphs on one of the clinical update sheets concerning a doctor in Tennessee who had arrested his lymphoma with the use of butyrates and something else...Was he a patient at the clinic? No, Dr. Bradford replied. He did it on his own. Dr. B. gives me the doctor's number in Knoxville. I called. Yes, almost ten years ago, now, he had lymphoma. My identical kind. The first day he saw a lump on his neck he had a biopsy done and presto-change-o he was at Mayo Clinic. It was hitting him bad. Mayo gave him four to six months. He went to Sloan-Kettering. Same thing. Why bother with chemo, said the doctors... it won't make any difference.

The doctor from Tennessee, one Dr. Cecil Pitard, an allergy specialist associated with the University of Tennessee School of Medicine got cracking with his own research and came up with a solution to his, and consequently many other cancer patients, problem. And here he was, almost ten years later, telling me what he did, about the other patients who have used this same procedure...and, no, of course there's no charge! He would never charge a cancer patient a dime! Just get my local doctor to fill out some prescriptions (all drugs safe, legal AND AVAILABLE IN THE U.S.A.!!!), give myself some shots, take some pills and that's it. It's a daily regime and will run about $300 a month for the drugs. He'll get a protocol (study with all the info) in the mail to me the next day. "Stay in touch," he says with a smile in his voice, "It's always great to hear how well my patients are doing!"

This treatment is called Conventional Biopharmacotherepy of Cancer. It's the fourth conventional modality of cancer treatment (in order of historic appearance) after surgery, radiation and chemotherapy. It consists of five drugs which, when used together, are said to create low cost, low technology, widely applicable, universally available, effective results. Plus, it can be used with other therapies as it's immunoprotective as well as immunorestorative. Sure, he says, a lot of doctors know about this. Success rate seems to be running in the 90-95 percent range. My, my, my, my, my. Imagine walking into a drugstore and asking for "One cancer kit, please!" His work has not been published yet in a medical journal, and media release prior to his publication could delay the work receiving wide acceptance by his peers. (I remembered the documentary on TV about the doctor who discovered AIDS was transferred to babies by their mothers. A press conference was held prior to his work being published in a medical journal and credibility dropped.)

Wednesday: X-rays. In-out. Tomorrow, results. Dentist tells me radiation could require most of my molars to be removed prior to treatment. Seems the saliva glands would be shot and the teeth would have problems and my bones would rot or some such thing!

Thursday: Well, well, well. The U ran my original biopsy slides and came up with a different diagnosis than Mayo Clinic. Oh, it's still lymphoma all right...except it's a different kind. But, hey, after all, who's perfect? But...who's right? Doesn't matter. Between the two I'm still in the same ball game, just different team. I'm still playing to win. It's getting a bit more intense. The localized lymphoma in the neck/collarbone area as per the Minnesota and the now-gone Mexico doctor and their "radiate" verdict is now: abdominal lymph node cancer. No, nothing new, it just hadn't been detected without the lymphangiogram. Radiation out...chemotherapy in. The good news is the head scan's fine. Dr. Pitard's protocol is on the way and I'm pumped full of Laetrile, vitamins and feeling good. Not to mention victorious.

To be told that friends and former co-workers were coordinating a benefit on my behalf was almost beyond comprehension. The outpouring of love and kindness has been so Incredible that I find it difficult to put into words.

When the company I worked for had to cancel their employees insurance in a belt-tightening move I, along with others, was hard hit. I discovered that for the last month and a half of tests, biopsy, "cat" scan and bone marrow tests I had no insurance. Nothing was covered! My friends, family and co-workers reacted to this with anger. They bore my anger for me as I couldn't afford to be angry. Time was too precious. Since I had been informed that the insurance company would have covered the alternative treatment I held fast to my conviction that if that was the way I was to go something would open up. It did. A loan was secured for me. Treatment was under way. My body was being given the best possible treatment from all sectors. All thanks to friends and family. And now this outpouring of community love. I raise my voice in praise!

Frankly, it's not like I was ever one to buck tradition, burn bras or riot in the streets. Heck, in the mid-60's I wore a pill box hat and white gloves. Nor was I a raging health fanatic rising out of some organic ooze lusting after vegetables and preservative free foods. I was just going on my way. Ups and downs, ins and outs and one day in my 45th year in Hotel Planet Earth I got cancer and something inside of me said, "Well, let's get this thing settled, shall we?"

For the past 40 years, the treatment of cancer has remained basically the same. Cancer increases annually. Cancer deaths increase annually. Honest to Pete...you'd think by now there would be something else around that has made an impact. I've found out there are other "things" around. I've also found out there's tremendous support from people to encourage seeking the best course of action. I pour my gratitude out on them all.

Next step: Back to the U. Get prescription filled. See how we progress. Chemo if necessary.

But, I don't know. I have a sneaky feeling about all this. A real good kind of sneaky feeling. I sense a change in the wind.

The Country
ECHO
Serving the Cass and Crow Wing County Lakes Area
35 CENTS

First, The Good News...

Cancer victim Jane Peters writes update

June-September, 1989

Sun., September 17: It's hard to imagine that 6 months ago today I was sitting in the doctors office getting the news that I had joined the ever-growing population of people testing positive for cancer.

During this time I've run the gamut from being so preoccupied with pill-taking and shot-taking that my bodily well being was all I could think of, to totally "knowing" I had a perfect physical self. Rather than jump into the traditional medical methods of cancer treatment I opted for the alternative route, including clinical treatment in Mexico with Laetrile and other vitamin therapy, plus the addition of a program from the University of Tennessee's Dr. Pitard. All non-toxic and all listed as "unproven".

But the options?

Chemotherapy is the only route for me to take as far as my doctors at the University of Minnesota are concerned...and they will be the first to admit that as long as I'm going the way I am there's no point in rushing into such a heavy duty course of action at this stage of the game. Matter of fact it seems that with or without chemo my projected "quality time" here on Planet Earth would be about the same. Well, now, doesn't take much for me to make a decision based on that!!

Not only that, I continue to receive information about treatment programs which are meeting with good success in other states. The one that I'm most interested in is the 2-Cda program from Scripps Clinic in California.

I've talked to my U. of M. oncologist and he has already sent a couple of his patients there. He told me not to judge by their results as they were not in the kind of "shape" I'm in...plus, the program is not open for people who have not had prior treatment (i.e. chemo, radiation) at this point. Come January, 1990, that is subject to change. The treatment is a non-toxic chemotherapy! Intravenous feeding for seven days in a row, off for 4 to 6 weeks, seven more days...on and off until "remission". Four or five sessions or so. Each patient is different, of course. It's been tested for the past 8 years and lymphoma patients are responding incredibly well. All I have to do is just keep holding on to my maintenance program and one day I will be as healed as I feel.

One of the benefits of being in Mexico is that I've been "networking" with some other patients. Blake, the songwriter from California, and his wife Lisa have been doing a lot of research on this 2-Cda program and I'm really just sort of riding on all their information. Neat couple. I'm hoping Blake gets to be the first "non-prior-treated" patient on this new treatment.

The good news is that I have had a decrease in my cancerous nodes. The bad news is that some new ones have sprung up! I feel fine other than tired, at times. But...I'm standing strong and confident that I have a lot to do before I write my final chapter and I'll be given the health and strength to accomplish what I'm to do! Perhaps best of all I've got a sound connection with my Impenetrable Life Within and the more I let that be "my" life the happier I feel.

Laughter has become a very vital aspect of my daily existence. Even when I don't feel like it I think about what's getting me "down" and look it straight in the eye and laugh at it. I mean guffaw, belly laugh. Try it! It may feel awkward at first, but something wonderfully freeing takes place! Books have been written regarding the validity of laughter as a healing agent, and, of course, Christians are told to laugh in the face of adversity time and time again.

My current regimen includes a ton of pills a day! (Well, how about 90 some-odd?!) A couple of shots every other day, another shot once a week, drops and a relatively strict diet. Sometimes I just rebel and ease up for a day or two. It gets so darn confining and all encompassing. Sometimes I get busy and forget and then I get the "guilts".

Busy doing what? Well, I embarked on a course of action basically to take care of unfinished business-projects which have been sitting on the drawing board, so-to-speak, for some time now. I've presented a TV station with a programming format which they're quite interested in and I should know the results in a couple of weeks; a major department store is reviewing a merchandising concept of mine; I'm coordinating a synopsis for a literary agent regarding a book which would be a resource/guide book to which cancer treatments are being offered where, and how to get information on them; and the ongoing daily affairs such as staying in touch with cancer patients I met in Mexico.

After calling two of my friends from the clinic and discovering one had died that day and the other was being buried the next, I decided not to make any more calls..."Just to say I had been thinking about them." I've discovered at least five have now made the transition to a truly cancer-free existence. Others are doing fairly well, considering so many of them had been so savagely attacked prior to starting the alternative treatment!

And then, wouldn't you know, on top of it all...I was minding my own business and into my life walked love! Well, actually, he was standing and I was walking next to the lake in Vergas, MN, the second Sunday in July. The annual "Fun in the Park" festival was taking place and I was enjoying the perfect summer day while bands played and hot dogs roasted. A gentle eyed, bearded man and I struck up a conversation. After a few minutes we went our separate ways, but before the day was through he reappeared and asked if we could "get together". My mom, my daughter and I were camping for the week at Rod and Shannon's in Detroit Lakes and the close proximity made it easy to say "I'd be delighted" to this Moorhead man.

The next couple of nights of well chaperoned dates made it evident I wanted to tell him of my "situation" before something was inadvertently revealed by mutual friends. Then again, should I tell him I had cancer...and I was, er, a decade or so older? Hmmmm. I figured the longer I put it off, the harder it would be. Well, seems he had lost his dearly beloved father to cancer in 1985. He was well aware of the devastation cancer wreaks on a life, having watched his articulate, handsome university professor father transform before his eyes in four short months. Transform from a vital, viable force of energy and strength into a non-recognizable, old, pain wracked man. His grandparents had been cancer victims, likewise a favorite uncle. Cancer was nothing new to him. After a few weeks of staying in touch he admitted he had been doubtful as to whether I would "beat" it, but he felt I would and wanted to give me whatever strength and support he could. And...as far as my being older? Well, it didn't matter to him if it didn't to me.

At times I've experienced a sense of hesitancy as to whether introducing a new relationship into my life was/is "fair". Heaven knows I'm not out-of-the-woods yet and having family and friends to be "concerned" about is enough without adding a romantic interest! However, who am I to quibble if love is "just what the doctor ordered". There's something magically restorative in that Power.

As it is I'm beginning yet another new course of action this week...acupuncture!! I don't know why it's taken me so long to get on THAT bandwagon. I've known about acupuncture treatment for the symptoms of lymphoma since the second week of my diagnosis...but for some reason I haven't acted on it until now. After all, I can get the treatments in Brainerd...and reasonably I might add! Of course, I'll keep doing what I'm doing as well.

I feel fine...people always say how "well" I look. The only time I get concerned is when I see the lumps on my neck, or feel them growing in my groin. At those time I just have to sit down...and have a good laugh! If they think they can scare me...they've got another think coming!!

The Country ECHO
Serving the Cass and Crow Wing County Lakes Area
35 CENTS

"The Beat Goes On..."

November 1990

This is incredible! Over a year since I've made my last journal entry! Can't believe it. Good thing I've been keeping notes.

Things are going well in my neck of the northwoods 19 months after I was first diagnosed as having non-Hodgkin's disease lymphoma.

Talk about running the gamut of emotions!

Initially I was led to believe I had an inoperable lymphoma which could only be treated with radiation and even with treatment I had an average "lifespan" of 8 years. Now I'm looking at my cancer "facts and figures" from a broader, wider... and, from my standpoint, better view.

First off, I don't have the kind of cancer we "first" thought I had.

Same ball park, different player and this one's a bit slower "growing" a bit less aggressive than the first one diagnosed. I like that kind of "error"; however, in the course of finding all that out, I've also been finding out a lot of other things! Neat things!! Exciting things that not only affect me personally but a heck of a lot of other people as well.

My personal choice of treatment to date has taken me to Mexico, into the alternative world of vitamins, Laetrile, homeopathy, and general "healthy lifestyle" attitude and nutrition. I'm on what's called a "Watch and Wait" program. That means every couple of months I see my oncologist; he checks my blood, feels my lumps and tells me to come back in "two...no make it three" months. He's a Big City doctor, who makes the northwoods rounds once a week and as far as he's concerned I seem to be doing OK. He's been aware of the route I've been taking to date and he's going to be the first to give me a frank, honest opinion..and it looks like his honest opinion is that as far as he's concerned I don't have to "rush" into treatment. By the time I got the second biopsy and opinion (way-back-when) the radiation treatment had become chemotherapy as the lymphoma was more wide spread than originally discerned. It was then that I found out (through the "alternative" network, I might add) about a non-toxic chemotherapy, 2-Cda, which was currently undergoing a clinical trial at Scripps Clinic in La Jolla. A non-toxic chemotherapy which worked best on lymphoma and leukemia patients. Didn't take too much to figure out what I wanted to do! Thanks once again to my INCREDIBLE friends and family I was winging off to the West Coast. First for a booster week at American Biologics clinic in Mexico and then on to Scripps Clinic for a "consultation."

March in Mexico found me returning to "Welcome Back, Juanita" and the comforting smiles of my clinic "family". This time around I noticed a difference.

There were more people using this as a first line of defense vs. a last line. I was an in-patient, experiencing a four-day fast as well as mega-dosages of vitamins, Laetrile, and live-cell therapy (shark, thank you).

From Mexico it was off to Scripps Clinic in La Jolla. There the doctors informed me I could be part of the 2-Cda clinical trial as long as I "lay off the funny stuff" for two months prior to treatment. They also said I was doing O.K. the way I was and if I wanted to keep on with the "watch and Wait" program, they had no objections. After all, lymphoma has been known to go into spontaneous remission! So, I got what I wanted: The option to use 2-Cda if/when desired. It had been a little "hairy" for awhile. I had been on Dr. Pitard's program which included Alpha-interferon, a treatment used in the U.S.A. for cancer but not the "accepted" treatment according to Scripps' guidelines. I had gotten real close to falling through a crack in the program...hence my trip to La Jolla. My friend, Blake, whom I had met the first time I was at AB was first to tell me about 2-Cda. I'm delighted to say he was the first "non-previously-treated" lymphoma patient in the program and he is now in a galloping state of remission.

My basic regime is pretty cut and dried: homeopathic drops, proper nutrition; visualization; maintenance vitamins/supplements. Last Fall I had gotten to a point where I was pilled, dropped and shot silly!! I'm talking 90 pills a day, a shot daily...that was too much for this lady. Then Don Heidt told me about an experimental homeopathic remedy that had some real impressive results. Well, needless to say the idea of putting one little drop in a glass of water eight times a day sounded a far cry better than what I was on...and besides, I needed a break. Two weeks after I began this program my "lumps" had decreased so much that even my doctor commented. I'm still taking Laetrile, but not in the amount as when initially diagnosed, and I drink my carrot juice. And then I drink some more. I've gotten information on Blue-Green Algae, so who knows what that will bring. I would just as soon continue to control the cancer in this manner...But, if for some reason, things aren't held in check the way they should be...I have an option or two for the choosing... and that's a nice feeling!

Speaking of great feelings!! The book is finished!! Do you remember the book I mentioned last time? Well, it's just about this side of being printed!! Called *Cancer: A Beginner's Guidebook of Hope* it's for people who have been recently diagnosed as having cancer. A quick, easy, ready-reference guide, so to speak. One which I hope will give readers a sense of reassurance, confidence...and most of all HOPE!! It's pretty much my "personal guide" suggestions as far as how to find what's going on in the traditional as well as the non-traditional medical treatment realm for cancer.

It's been incredible how the book has come together and how many people are directly and indirectly responsible. John Plein and Mary Plein of Golden Oaks Graphics have been invaluable in the final "birthing process"; Paula Schaub and Polly Susens encouraged, listened and loved. Liz Dean is such a great friend that she can be a critic without hurting my feelings; Kenny Oaks didn't realize it but he provided a great opening line in the introduction; and the owners and editor of the Country Echo first gave me the opportunity to "feel better...more alive!" by sharing my experience. If finishing the book hasn't been gratifying enough, four songs co-written by me have been included on the album *See it Thru* by the Minnesota progressive "neon country" band, Glass House...and to top it off, *Harbor of Your Arms*, the theme song from my continuing work-in-progress, *Mary Rockopera* was an award winner in the 1990 Nashville Music City Song Festival. Now, folks round this neck of the woods know that Jane's been real happy about all of this and so on...but the facts are it's still business as usual. While working on the book, p.m.'s, I had fun waitressing a.m.'s in the Marina Restaurant at Breezy Point. Good to be around all my old/new cohorts. I'm still doing some freelance writing now and again and, yessireesir, I'm taking all that good info I've been absorbing and turning it into the *Health Nut Cafe* column.

It's been a pretty eventful time. An eye opening year. It hasn't been all sweetness and light, though. Although I rejoice with gladness beyond comprehension when I witness friends and community members rally from cancer there is sadness for the families of loved ones who have not survived the struggle. I live in a part of the world where community spirit and love ignites the heart. A part of the planet where love, time, energy and money is put into waging a successful campaign against cancer. I'm very fortunate to be a witness to this.

Yes, the past year I've seen love beyond description. (The long-distance "summer love" was too long distance). The love I'm referring to is the love I saw walking, talking, living and breathing in family, friends, community members and strangers who have encouraged me with emotional, as well as financial, support. The healing power in the on-going prayers, gentle touch and unspoken words has been, and is, the most precious gift imaginable.

What if I had taken the "traditional" route from the very beginning? Would I feel better? Worse? I don't know the answer to that. What I do know is the course I've chosen has been the right one for me. I've been able to take time to chart my course. Now it's onward and upward. One thing's for certain: early detection is best...prevention is BETTER

A new "me" is growing daily. Norman Cousins, in his book *Head First* writes, "Far more real than the ticking of time is the way we open up the minutes and invest them with meaning. Death is not the ultimate tragedy in life. The ultimate tragedy is to die without discovering the possibilities of full growth."

I, for one, have a lot of minutes to open! Yes, "the beat goes on...!"

Chapter Seven

In Summary

I hope, at this point, you are feeling more hopeful...reassured...comforted. There is a wealth of information out there but you do have to make phone calls, read books and talk to people. Digest well what you hear and read. Then, armed with your self-information begin to step, no, MARCH into the course of action which is best for you.

Remind yourself daily that you are now a member of a huge tribe of people attempting to control their cancer. Begin to gain strength from knowing that you DO have control over much more than you may have at first realized: What thoughts you choose to think..what course of action you choose to follow...even what foods you choose to eat! It's ironic that something as emotionally paralyzing as cancer can result in your finding an overwhelming sense of freedom.

By virtue of the fact that you have cancer you are being introduced to a here-to-fore unknown world consisting of medically accepted clinical trials and research programs as well as alternative therapies such as live-cell therapy, metabolic, macrobiotic and the like. You will speak to people who believe Laetrile is the best thing to come down the pike and others who don't. You will discover what visualization is all about, "laugh" therapy and anti-stress techniques.

Welcome to the world of herb teas and faith healing. Colonics and laser surgery. In the process you will meet people who have run the gamut of surgery, chemotherapy, radiation and are alive and well to talk about it. You will also meet others who say they dearly wished they had tried alternative treatment first as "standard" treatment has been unsuccessful. You will speak with or read about people who have only gone the "alternative route" and have been medically diagnosed as "cancer free"...or originally misdiagnosed. Spontaneous remission will be mentioned as something that does, sure enough, happen. Even doctors will speak of a miracle healing. Too often you will speak with or hear of family and friends who only wished their loved one had not "jumped" right into traditional treatment...but no one knew there were choices!

After all, they'll say, "what do you do?" Well, what you do is what YOU are doing! You explore the possibilities. You discover the optional treatment within the accepted treatment circles. You request information from alternative treatment centers. You do your homework. Notice I said "YOU" because from here on out it is completely up to you, and if possible or necessary, your support crew. This book is just a general sampling of what-to-do's and where-to-go's. I hope what you find is comforting and fruitful.

In closing I would like to add a personal word of thanks:

Thank you dear family, friends, community members and strangers alike for all the love, prayers and encouragement. Thank you, doctors, researchers, cancer/control laymen and women, hospitals and clinics for your dedication and perseverance. Thank You, Dear God, for them. And, God, thank You for the Lovely Gift of Your Son so that I "shall not perish but have everlasting life." (John 3:16) You are one Wonderful Creator!!

From Jane,
with love

Notes

It is our hope that this guidebook will bring helpful insight to those who face seemingly unsurmountable obstacles in their health, in their happiness and in their faith.

Cancer: A Beginner's Guidebook of Hope was produced using state of the art electronic publishing techniques. Our mission is to bring these advances within reach of small businesses and organizations.

Feel free to send questions, comments or requests for additional copies.

John and Mary Plein

Golden Oaks
GRAPHICS

Hc 83 Box 745 ❖ Ideal Corners, MN ❖ 56472 ❖ (218) 543-6479

About the Author

A number of months after being diagnosed as having inoperable non-Hodgkin's disease lymphoma Jane Peters said "I just wish I knew then what I know now!" Realizing how options can appear limited for the newly diagnosed cancer patient, Jane wrote *Cancer: a Beginner's Guidebook of Hope* to help broaden horizons and provide information for others facing a similar challenge.

The result of two writers, Jane was raised and educated bi-coastally and in Europe. Sometimes married, sometimes not; sometimes employed, sometimes not; her personal life has rivaled the extreme highs and lows of a Minnesota thermometer. Jane's theme: "Communication from the Heart" is echoed in her writing, songwriting, performance art and graphic designs. She is the original creator of the "From...with love" logo which began in 1979 as "From Minnesota...with love" featuring a heart bearing loon.

The current chapter of Jane's life finds her a "hardworking, garden variety, single mom of a teenage daughter living temporarily under her mother's roof in the northwoods of Minnesota." She continues to communicate with her column, *Health Nut Cafe*, in the local weekly and songwriting.